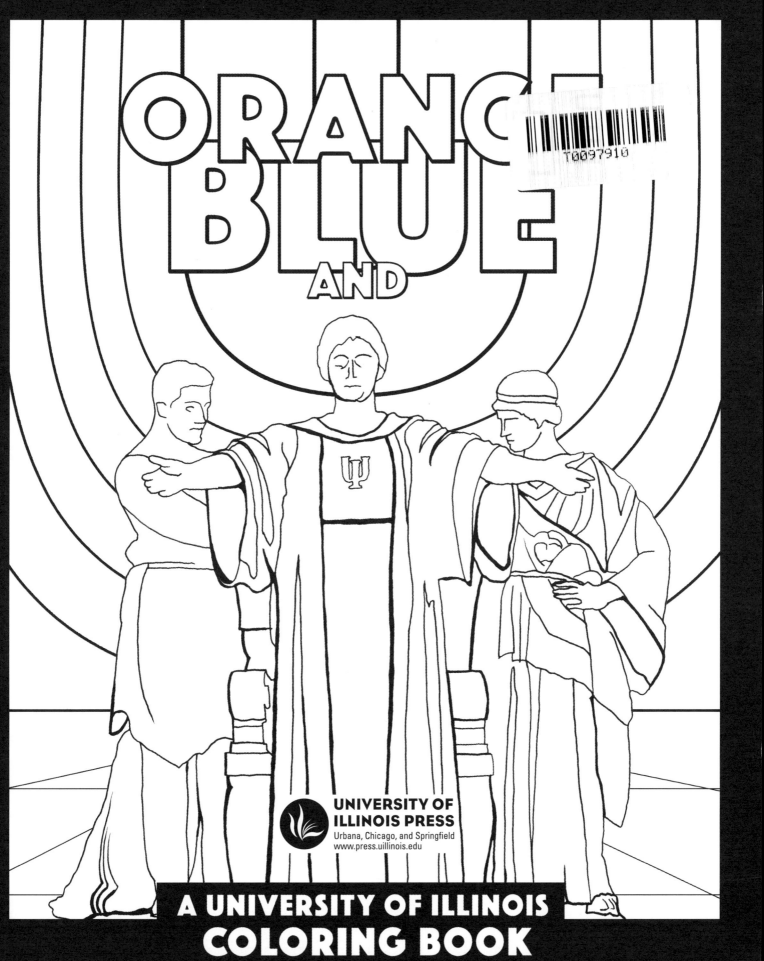

ORANGE BLUE AND

UNIVERSITY OF ILLINOIS PRESS
Urbana, Chicago, and Springfield
www.press.uillinois.edu

A UNIVERSITY OF ILLINOIS
COLORING BOOK

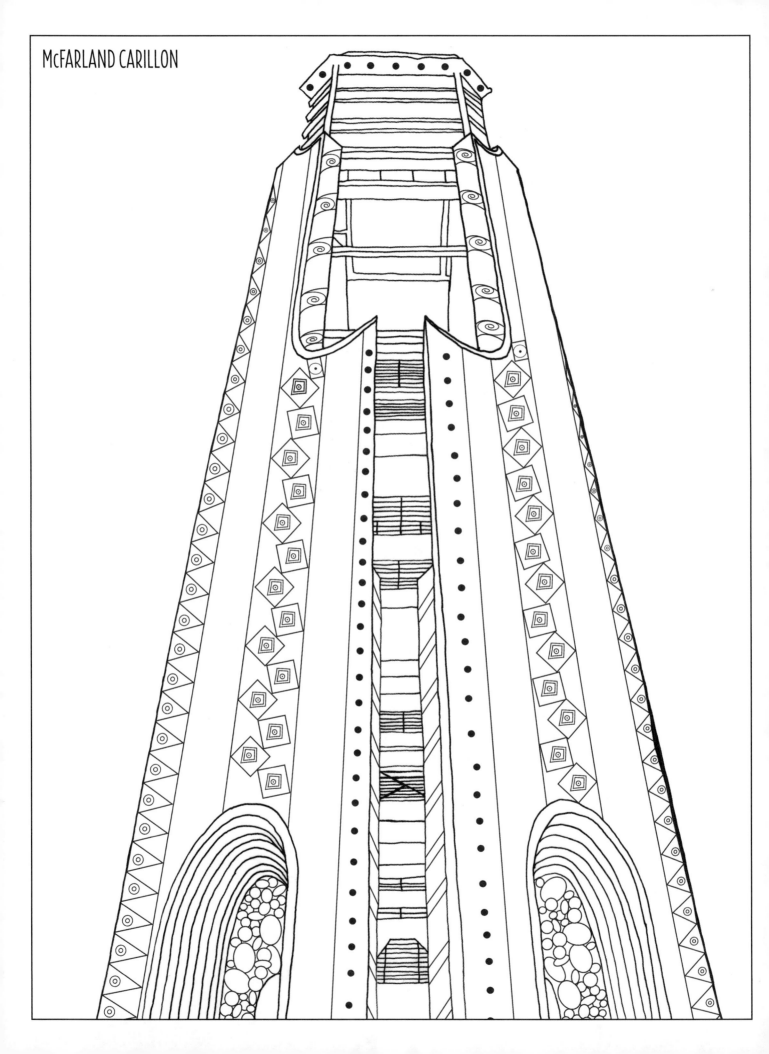

McFARLAND CARILLON

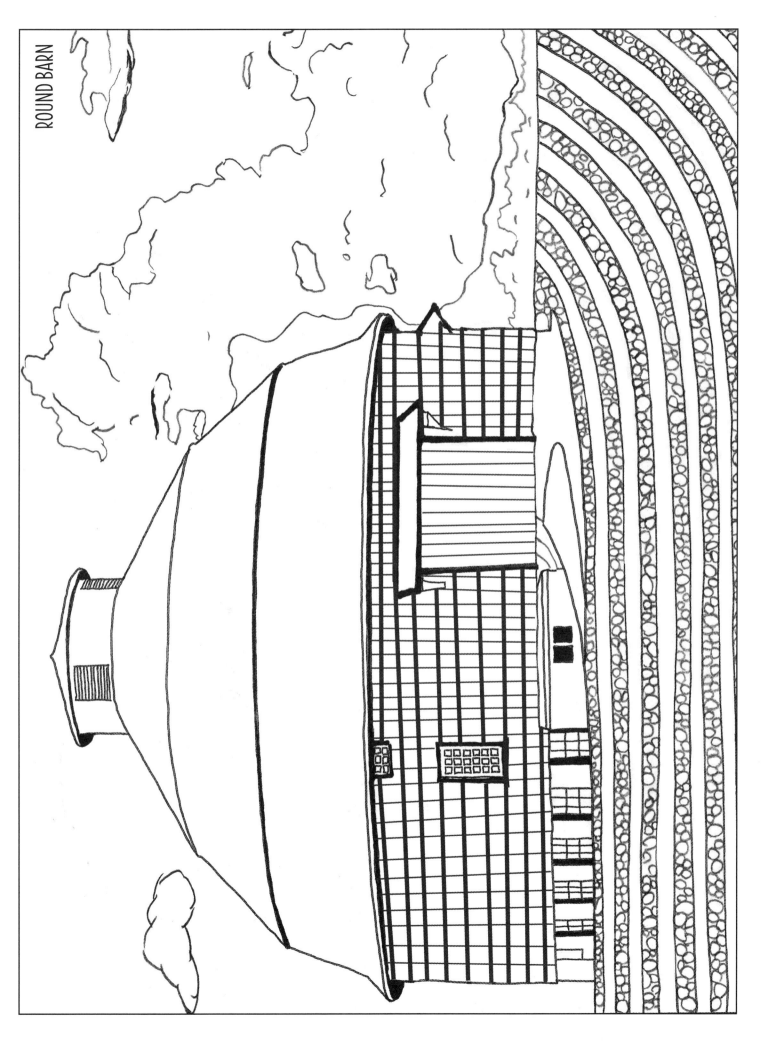

ROUND BARN

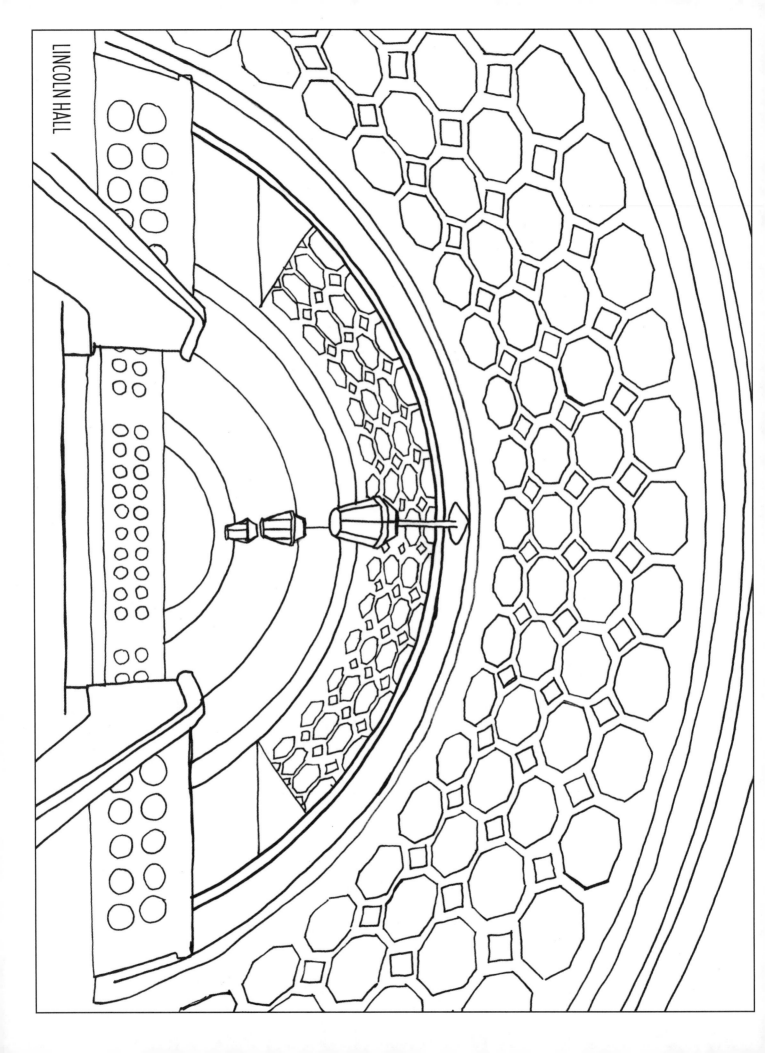

LINCOLN HALL

IDEA GARDEN TOPIARY

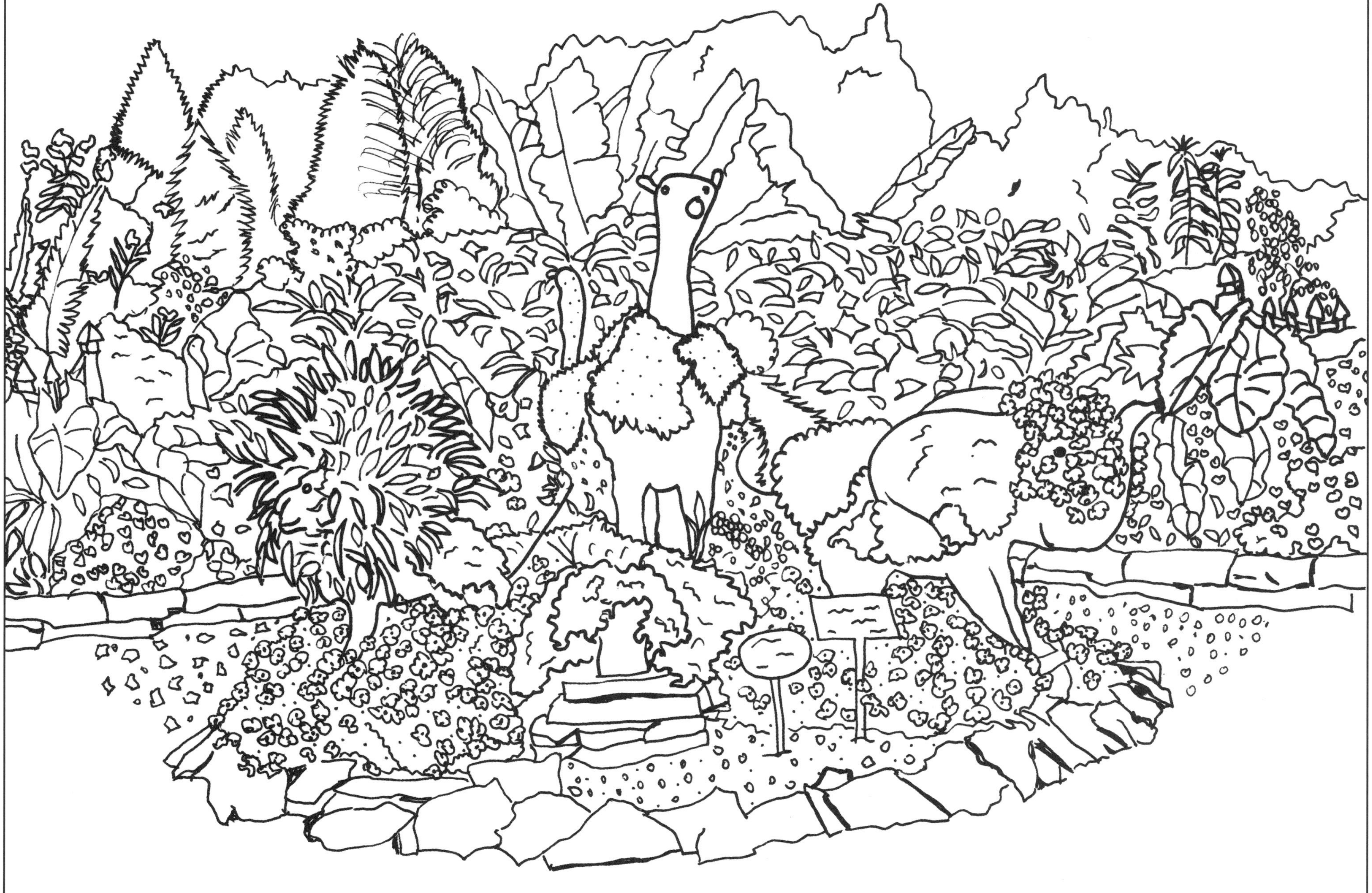

RED GRANGE AND MEMORIAL STADIUM

HALLENE GATEWAY

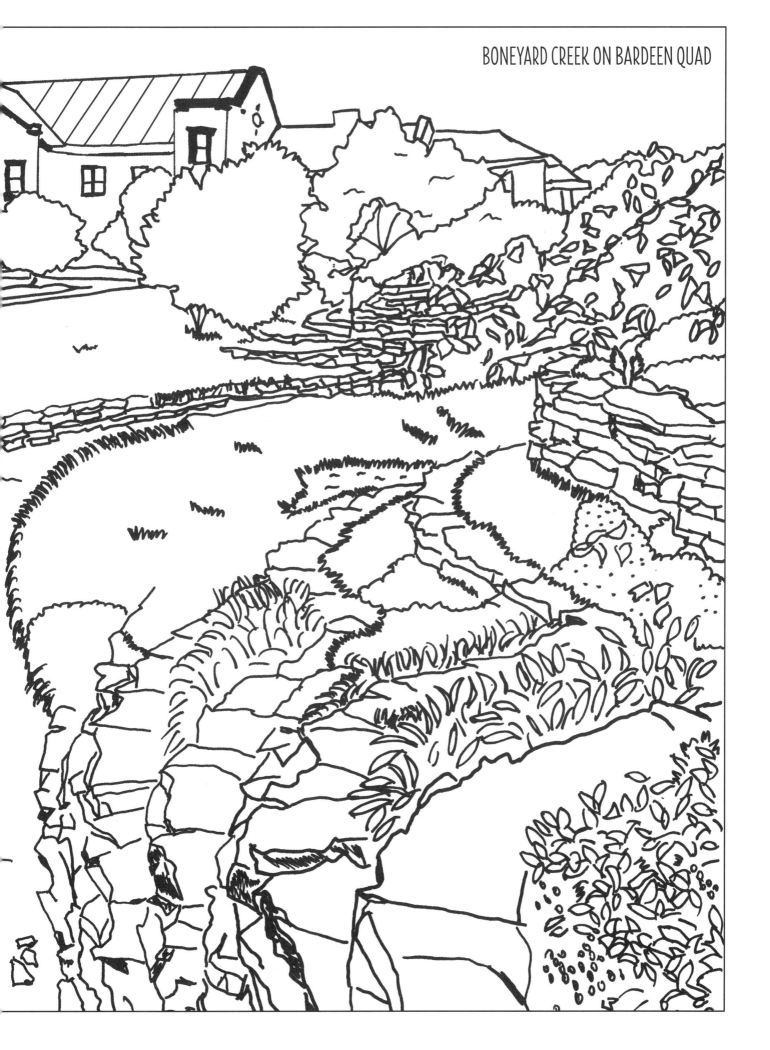

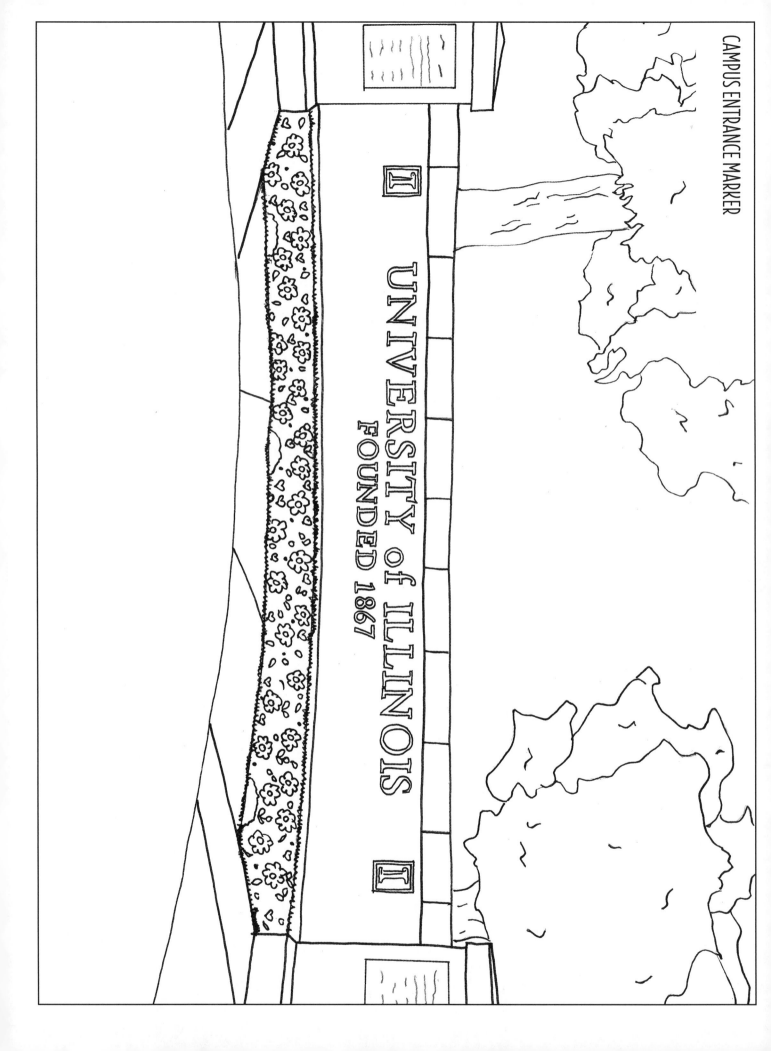

UNIVERSITY of ILLINOIS
FOUNDED 1867

ILLINI UNION CUPOLA

STATE FARM CENTER

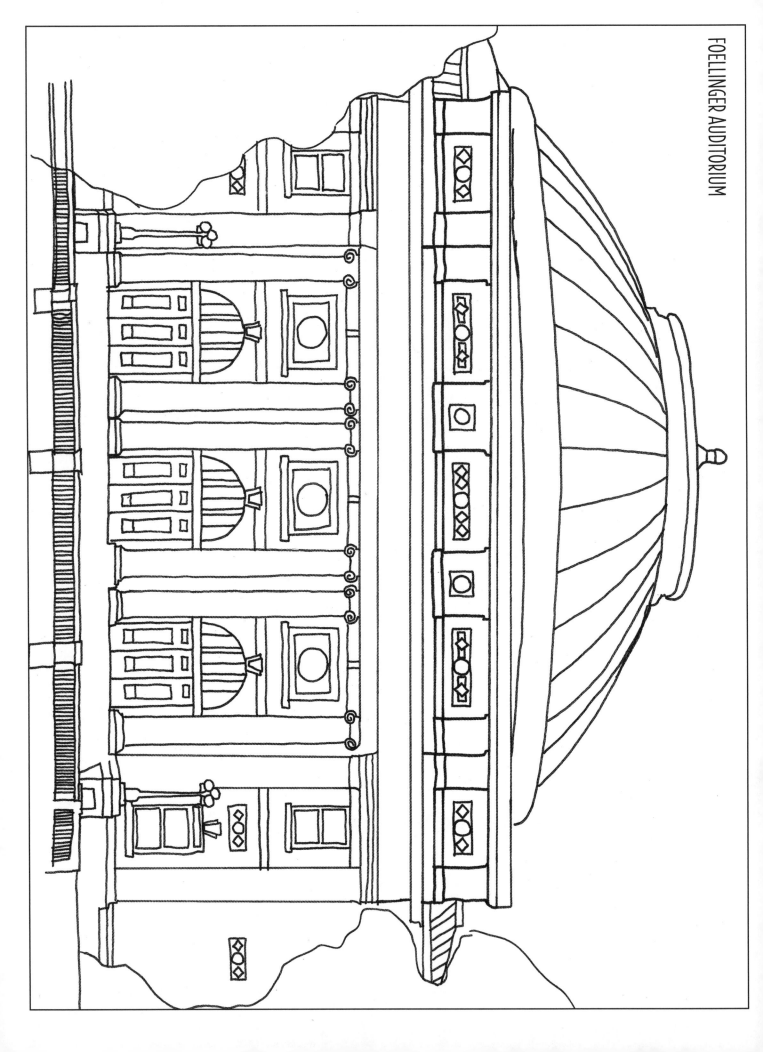

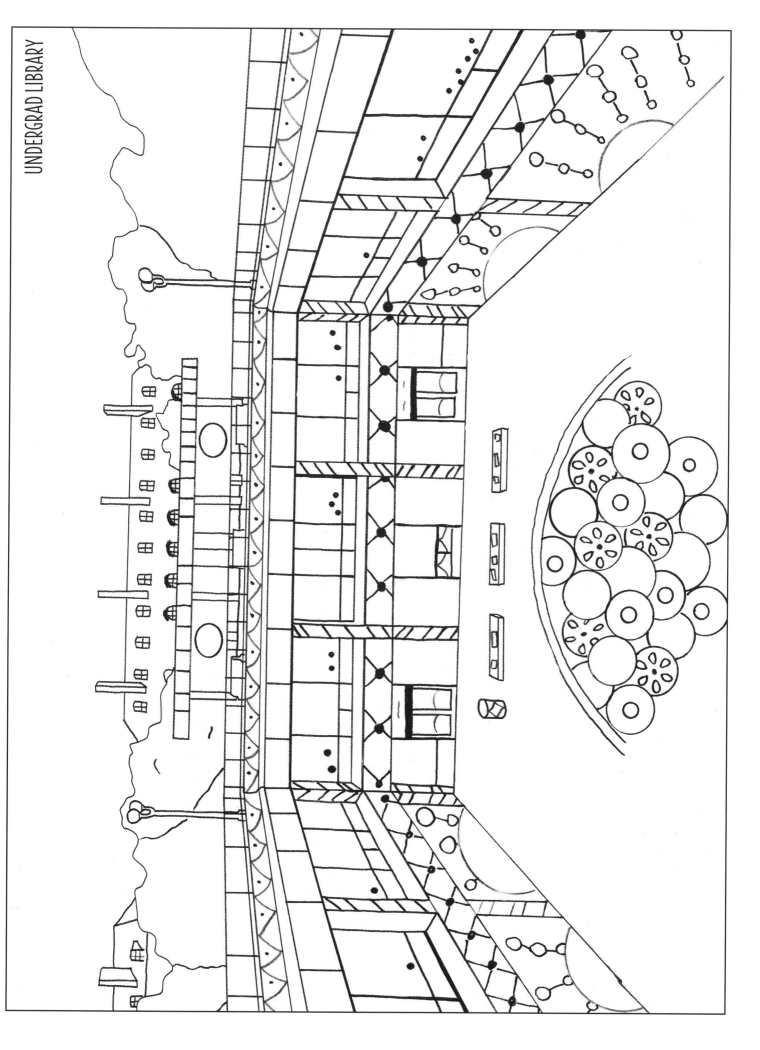

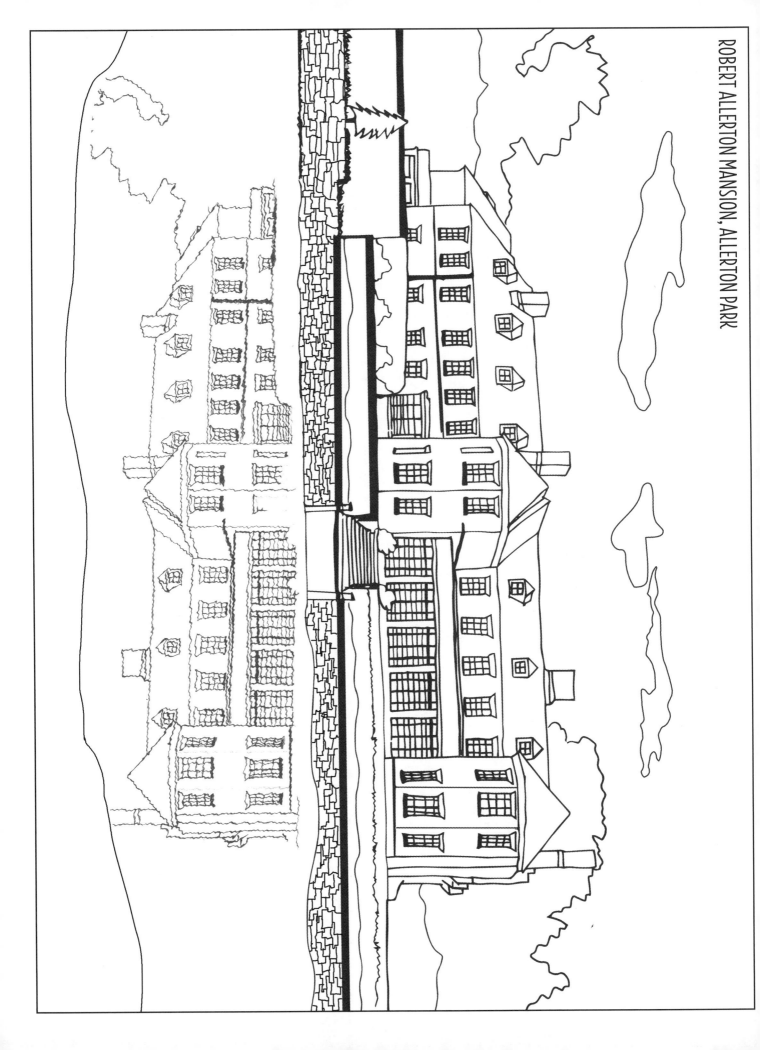

INNER GARDEN, JAPAN HOUSE

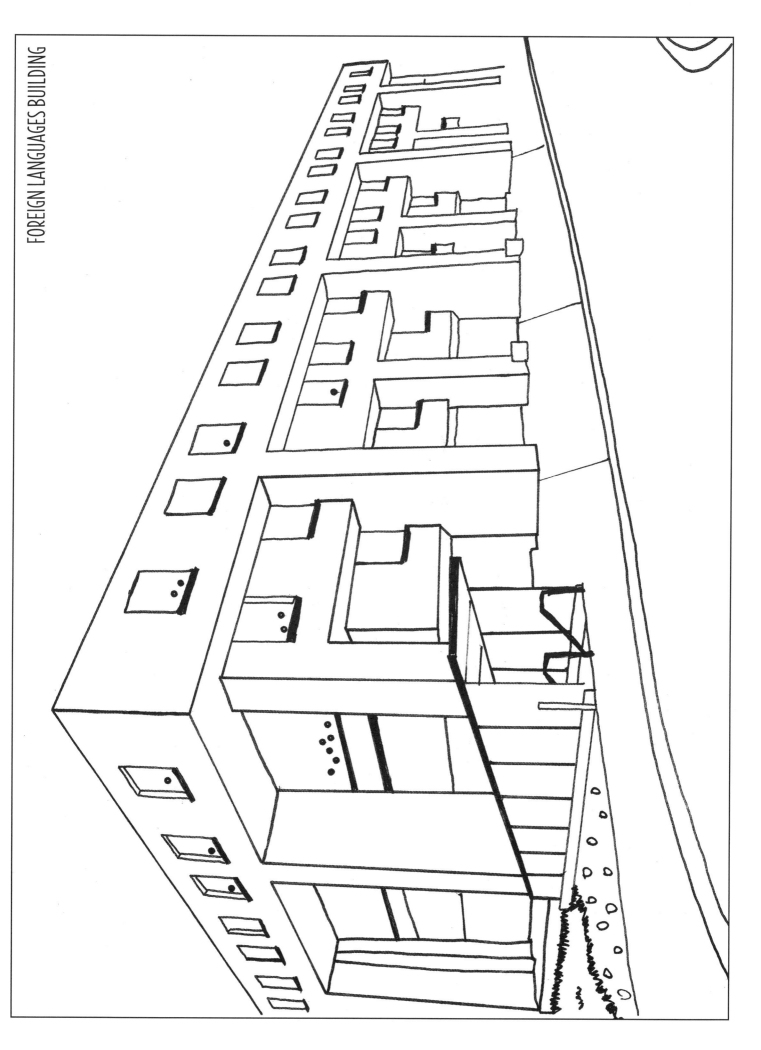

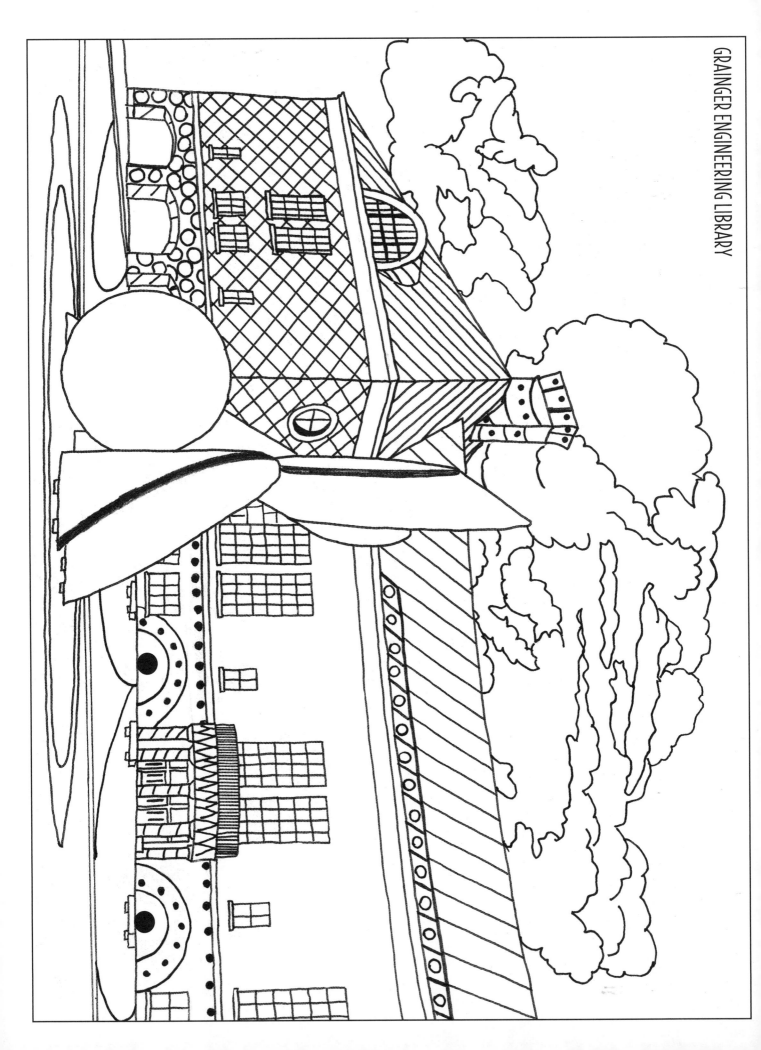

OBSERVATORY

MEMORIAL STADIUM SCOREBOARD

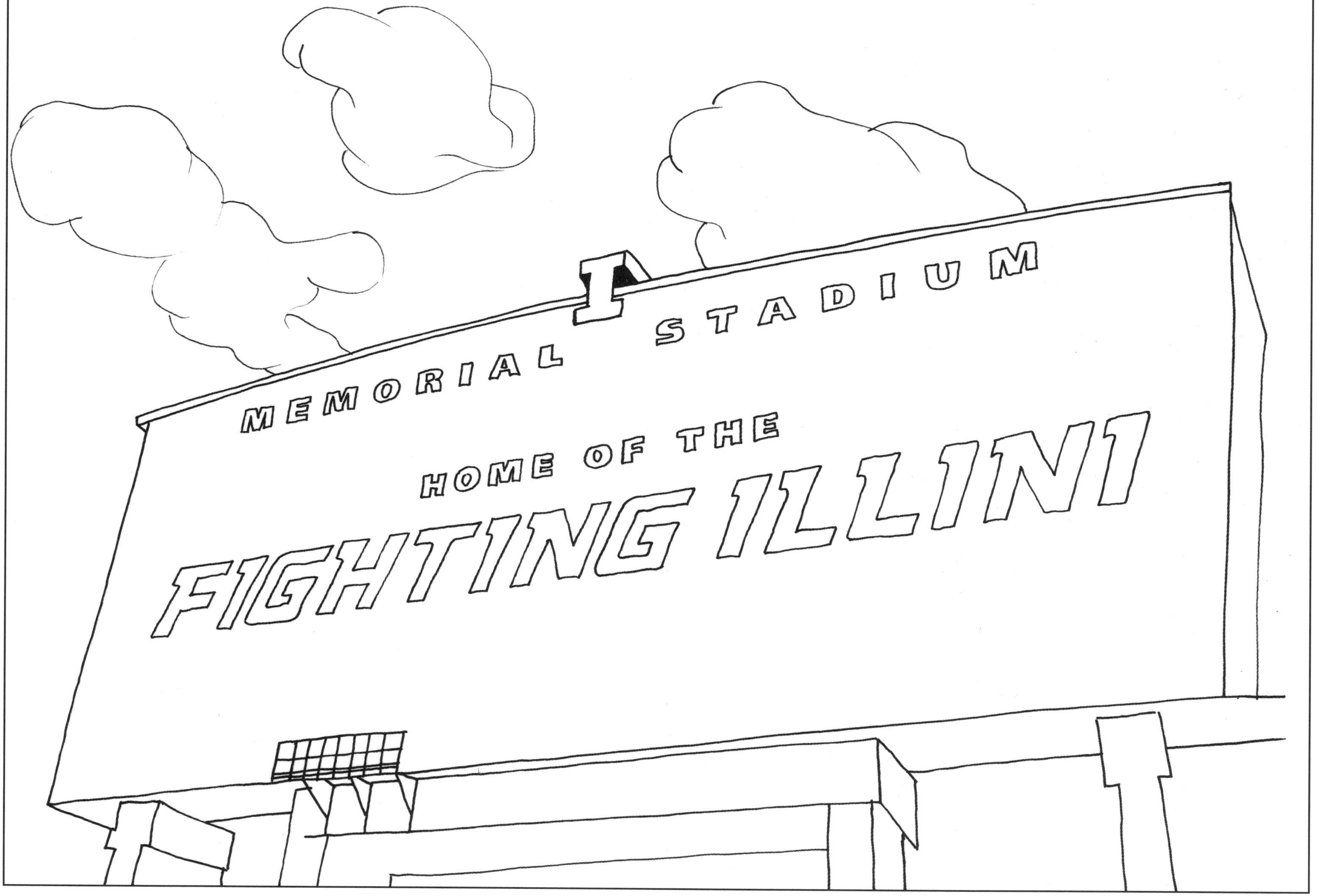

BUST OF ABRAHAM LINCOLN IN LINCOLN HALL

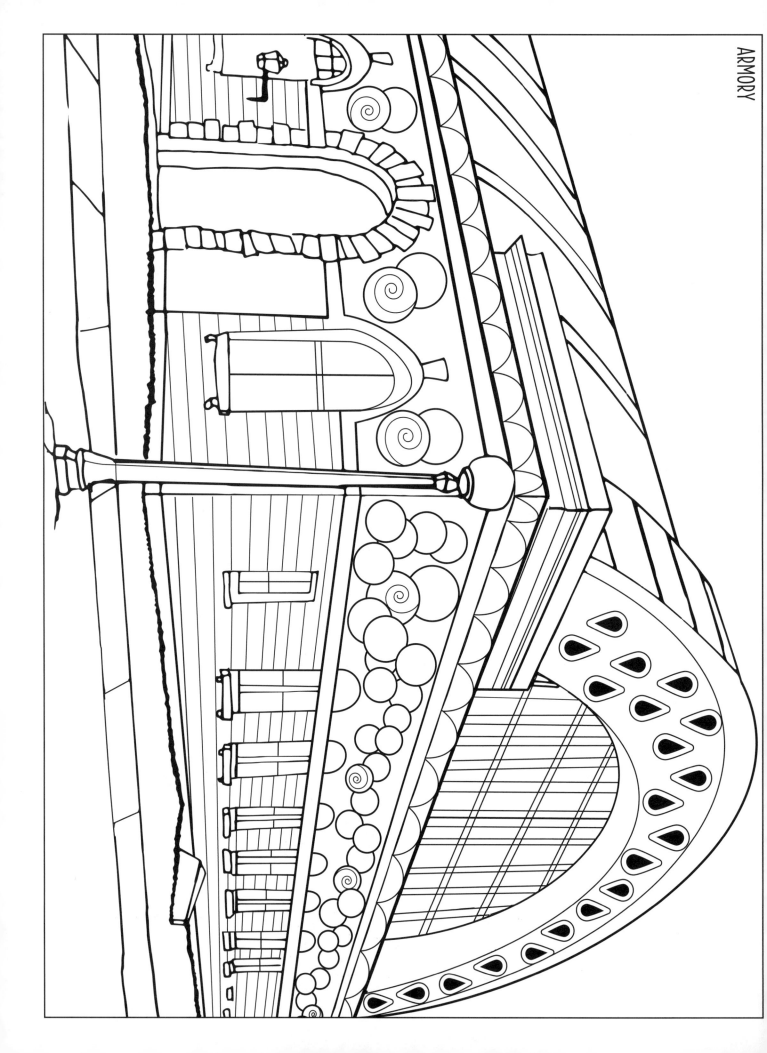

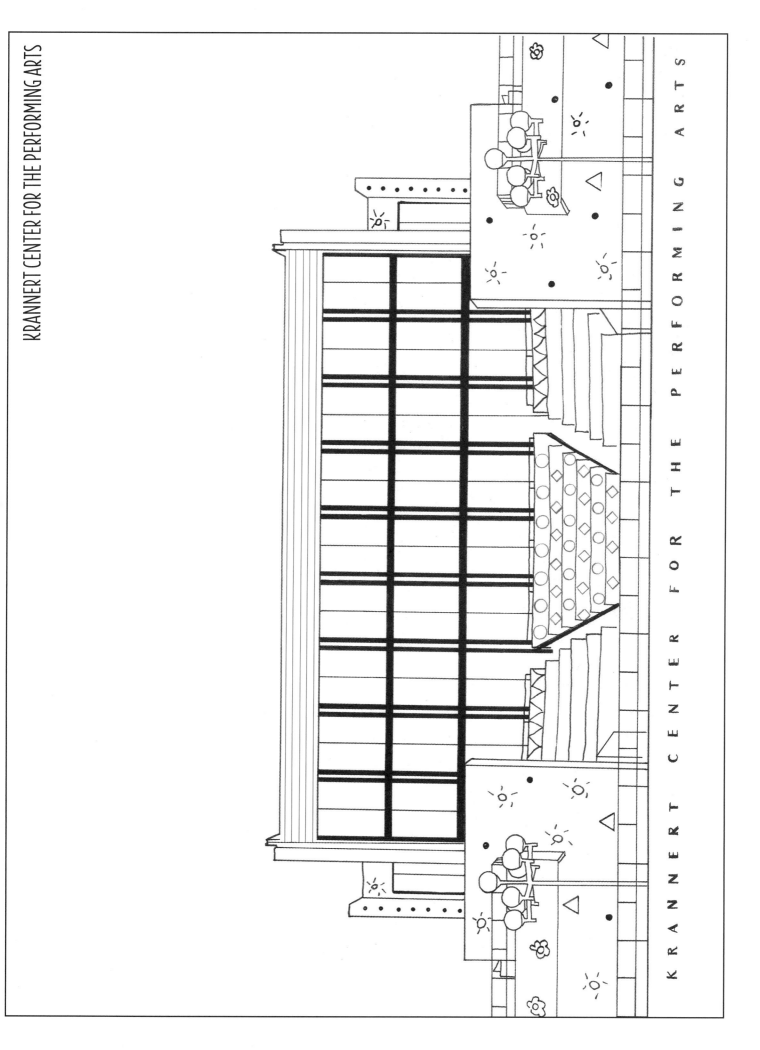

KRANNERT CENTER FOR THE PERFORMING ARTS

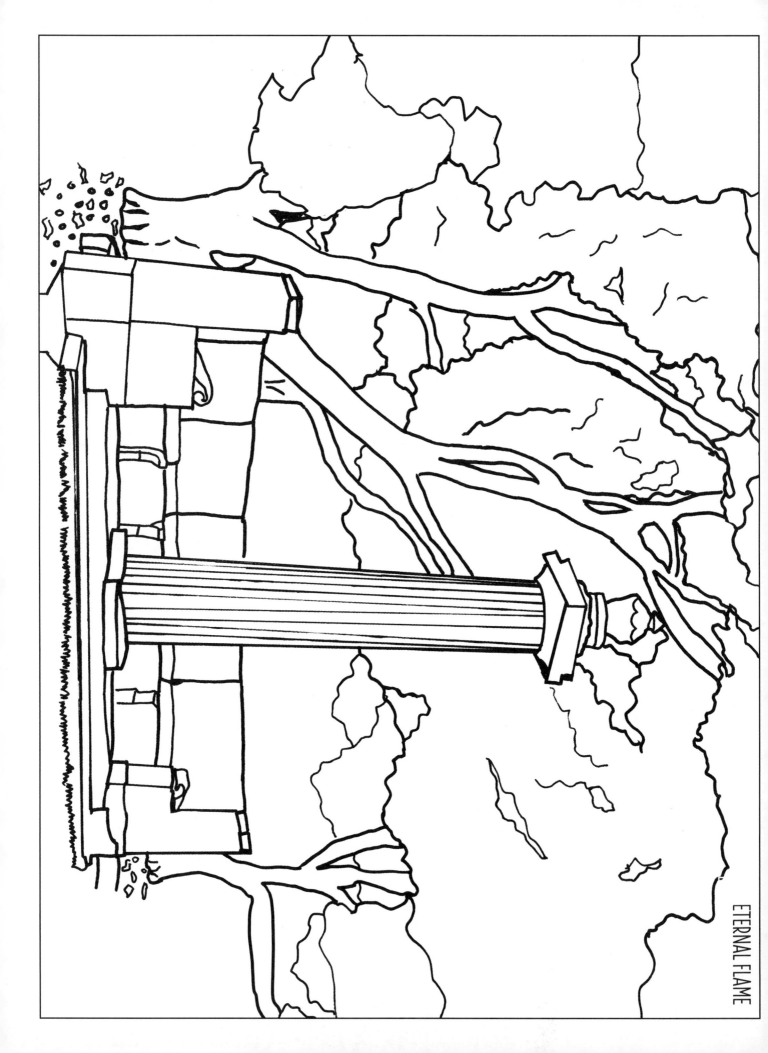

ETERNAL FLAME